THE
RACE
TO THE TOP

How to Take Over the Social Media Feed

By Jonathan Goodman

To my Mom and Dad

Introduction

This book was written as a continual stream of thought. It's meant to be read in 1 sitting. You will feel like you're racing through the pages (pun definitely intended). I want you to try and read through the entire book in one sitting. Shut off all distractions and engulf yourself in it.

After your first read-through you will gain a superficial overview of the theory. Your head will be spinning and you'll want to apply the concepts immediately to your business. The information contained within this book is powerful. It has the ability to take your idea or product and make it dominate the field while gaining you expert status.

Slow down.

I want you to read over the book a second time 2-4 days later. This time have a notebook beside you or write directly in the margins of the book. Look deeply into the examples I gave and understand that they're just that, examples. Write down ideas of how you would take the concept behind the examples and apply it to your business.

Read the book a page at a time and think critically about each section before moving onto the next. The sections are short but were carefully written. Think about each word and example I gave and why I chose them.

We're in an age of unlimited opportunity. Never before has it been so cheap and easy to get your message out and scale your marketing. It doesn't make much you just have to know where and how to focus your efforts. Luckily, you've come to the right place.

Now fill your cup of coffee (or scotch), put your feet up, and enjoy…

THE
RACE
TO THE TOP

Greg Ohnoez is one of my most important followers. He's not well-known or particularly well-connected. For as long as I've known him his Facebook profile picture has been a Buddha. When I spoke to him he even told me that his real name wasn't Greg Ohnoez, it's Greg O'Hare. I don't know what he looks like and, until recently, didn't know his real name. Yet I have Greg O'Hare to thank for a lot of my success.

Greg's not a personal trainer but he's somebody who's avidly interested in fitness. Out of nowhere he entered the internet fitness community and made an impact. He uses his blog as a diary – as a way to organize his thoughts. He doesn't care if anybody else reads it which is largely why people do. Through Facebook Greg plays a large part in how information spreads through the fitness community. He gives power to many of the top figures in a powerful industry and he doesn't even know he's doing it.

Greg's goal is not to become famous and it's not to sell a product or service. He's a consumer and isn't embarrassed to admit it and broadcast it.

When Greg likes somebody or something he shares it - interact with Greg and he'll interact back. Show Greg O'Hare that he's important and he'll go out of his way to make sure his World knows who you are.

If your goal is to make an impact then find your own Greg O'Hare – my guess is he's been right under your nose the whole time.

Fitness is a Game

Fitocracy.com is blowing up. At 275,000 users still in their Beta version they're about to finally release their iPhone App. With it they intend to reach 1,000,000 users in 6 months time. I bet it doesn't even take them that long.

Workout trackers on the internet are nothing new. Exercisers enter in how long they ran or how much weight they lifted into a computer program. Depending on the software the program then graphs the results.

Richard "Dick" Talens and Brian Wang like video games – a lot. They spent their childhood trying to "level up" their characters. This was the impetus for Fitocracy, to turn it into a game. But that wasn't the brilliant part.

What Dick and Brian did was build what Seth Godin describes as a tribe. They made the game nerdy and went after all the workout buffs that spent their childhood levelling up in Zelda and Super Mario Brothers. They included fun quirks like the "props" button instead of the Facebook "like". Achievements are unlocked with names like "Psycho Cycler" and the truly brave can attempt harrowing quests like the "Advanced Widowmaker".

Exclusivity strengthened their tribe by giving each user invite codes to get their friends to join. The members already playing felt special because they had a code to give out and went out of their way to tell their friends.

They recruited an expert team but it wasn't who you'd expect. Dick and Brian went straight after the obscure bloggers with large dedicated followings. They didn't bother with the usual industry experts.

Fitocracy is in the driver's seat in a competitive niche because it appealed to the obscure. What has your company done to give people a reason to care?

Carpenter Ants

You don't see carpenter ants. They prefer moist wood and usually reside in decks and porches. They dig nests in the wood and cut out galleries so they can move from nest to nest. Aside from being pests and occasionally leaving some sawdust around, carpenter ants don't do much real damage.

They just exist.

They use your home and never say thank you. Without you (or people like you) they wouldn't have a place to live.

I Was a Carpenter Ant

For 2 years I secretly hollowed out blogs and didn't even think about giving anything back. I never "liked" shared, or tweeted a thing. It never crossed my mind to send a thank you note to the author and I never bought a thing from the site.

Groggily I'd wake up and put oil in the frying pan. As it heated I would turn on my computer and open my favourite fitness blogs. I perfected the technique of using one hand to eat my eggs so my other hand would stay clean to use the mouse.

Like a sponge I absorbed and adapted much of what I read. Without the blogs my career would be years behind where it is now. When I did buy books I didn't think to click through on the link provided so the author didn't get a commission.

Most readers of your information are carpenter ants and they're hollowing you out from the inside. Without you they wouldn't survive, yet they don't give you anything in return.

Whether you're blogging for a multi-national company, a small neighbourhood branch, or to improve your personal brand, carpenter ants are there. That's fine – you're helping them. Problem is with only them you won't survive. Your information will never spread to the ones who will buy your products or pay to see you speak in person.

The Influencer

Joe Dowdell is a celebrity. These days it's hard to pick up a fitness magazine and not see his name. When he shares an article via Facebook or Twitter it instantly gains credibility and a flurry of activity follows.

Joe owns a gym called Peak Performance in New York City which was ranked the 3rd best gym in America by Men's Health in 2011. Additionally Joe is writing 1-2 books at a time and is prominent on the speaking circuit.

As a result Joe doesn't have time to read blogs. He's found information providers that he trusts in the industry and makes a point to support them. If somebody he trusts suggests he read a blog by another author he'll have a look.

Industry celebrities are busy people and are being pulled in 1001 different directions. Usually they handle email correspondence and their social networks personally which stretches their time even further.

When Joe posts an article or something about his life on a social network he receives at least 20 replies. It's impossible for him to respond to each and to remember each person who wrote them. Instead he chooses a couple key questions and responds to those. The same goes for email. When an email inbox is flooded, the last thing anybody in Joe's position has time or energy to do is read through your 1,500 word blog post. There just aren't enough hours in the day.

I'm not suggesting you don't connect with industry celebrities. Joe is one of the nicest and most genuine guys I've met and I'm proud to call him a friend. I also know for a fact that he reads all his emails and is constantly frustrated that he doesn't have time to reply to everybody as thoroughly as he'd like.

What I do suggest is that you're going about gaining influence the wrong way. Why work endlessly attempting to get a celebrity to share your material when the hungry are right under your nose?

The Sea Lion

My family was on a little fishing boat in the middle of Alaska. The water was calm when out of the blue birds started to congregate in one place. All of a sudden the sonar under our boat started broadcasting whale calls. Bubbles formed at the top of the water and 15 whales shot out. The once calm idyllic setting turned into a flurry of activity with whales getting most of the krill fish.

What most wouldn't have noticed were the sea lions. The sea lions stayed on the outside of the chaos and caught the fish that the whales left behind or flung too far away. They knew that by following the whales they'd have dinner.

Sea lions in Alaska are opportunistic.

Celebrities like Joe have done the work for you. His appeal and widespread respect has congregated lots of like-minded people in one place. When he posts on Facebook or Twitter it starts a flurry of activity similar to a bubble feed.

Why not follow the sea lions' example?

Instead of trying to get the attention of the influencer during a bubble feed, why not use it as research. Pay attention to those commenting and liking the influencer's post. These are your targets -- not the influencer.

I found Greg O'Hare by being a sea lion. He commented on 3 straight posts from 3 different influencers on the same day. It was obvious from the start that he was the type to actively participate and spread information.

Success is achieved by finding those that are willing and eager to share, comment, and "like" your work. Not everybody will despite your best efforts. The trick is to find your Greg O'Hares.

This book will show you how to attract, appeal to, and foster relationships with those who will share your info. It will teach you how to write and market material that's shareable irrelevant of your business type and size.

Wouldn't it be nice to never advertise again?

The Race to the Top... of the Feed

I predict the feed will be the most important marketing tool moving forward. Those at the top will become the go-to sources for information in their community, their industry, and the world.

Miss out on the feed and you'll be pushed aside, not just from people's minds but also from their wallets.

I believe:

- Referral traffic to websites will continue to grow making SEO (Search Engine Optimization) less valuable.

- Those who understand why individuals share via social media will develop into industry experts earlier and with fewer credentials than ever before.

- Professional accounts don't dominate feeds. Large organisations will be forced to become more personal if they hope to win the race to the top.

- The #1 reason why information doesn't share is because it's high quality. Nobody wants to read a textbook online and people shy away from sharing information that they don't already know.

- Information is shared for 3 main reasons:

  1. It's funny / nice to watch (usually useless to the creator)

  2. The person sharing wants to become part of a group or strengthen their position within one.

3. The person sharing is either consciously or sub-consciously using the information as a tool to boast about their own activities. (Not a bad thing)

The feed is everything. It's where you should focus all of your resources. The world is entering an age it's never been in before. Information is free and easy to attain. Minds will be saturated hearing about your product or service (if they haven't already). The feed is the only source of information anybody cares about anymore for one simple reason:

Users trust the people providing it.

Loved ones dominate our feeds. When they link to a movie trailer you watch it when you'd otherwise skip the commercial. When they tag a blog post as "something I found interesting" you read it more thoroughly than you would if you came across the same article via an organic search.

The race to the top of the feed is the most important aspect of your business. Gain access to it before anybody else in your industry and you'll cement your position as a leader. Don't fall into the trap of being conventional. Conventional doesn't work anymore because nobody will listen to you. Content has become secondary to context. This is your chance.

You're Doing It All Wrong

Want to make yourself the expert? Stop trying to appeal to potential customers.

Future customers don't care about you now. You need to stay in the feed long enough for them to find you when they need your product.

The way to stay in the feed is to appeal to people already using your product or working in your industry. The primary reason why people share your information (and your name) is to show off what they already do or know.

You're giving them a tool to project their own thoughts when they're not comfortable doing it themselves. Do so and you'll quickly become the expert. People like it when their thinking is justified by somebody else and they'll share it as a way to show off what they already know. This should be your goal.

Package people's thoughts well so they will want to show your information off as an extension of themselves.

Jon Goodman is...

Remember when Facebook status updates were really about what you were doing at that point in time? They forced the word "is" after your name.

How about Facebook groups? Remember them? Lots of companies do. Businesses spent piles of money building up their group members before Facebook decided to change to the professional page format in October, 2010. Group members weren't transferred to the new pages and millions of customer leads were lost by companies around the world.

Pages gave companies the opportunities to design Apps. This started a new industry of Facebook App design and the race to get the best landing page was on. Lo and behold, Facebook decided to change its page format to a timeline on March 30, 2012. Apps were pushed to the side and their effectiveness went way down.

Facebook, Twitter, Linkedin, and Foursquare will change. Companies like Pintrest will pop up and try to make their mark. If you try to keep up with all of the current trends and software you'll go nuts. Lucky for you it doesn't matter.

All you need to know is the answer to one simple question, "Why do people share?" It doesn't matter whether they "like", "tweet", "email", "check in" or "pin". The concept is the same. People are projecting where they are and what they like. The trick is to make them speak about you using whatever means they have.

In this book I use a lot of examples from the fitness world. It's my background and what I know best. Understand they're only examples. The concepts carry over to almost every industry on both small and large scales.

There are 3 types of people that are going to read this book:

1. People who don't think for themselves. They'll take my examples at face value and use them immediately after reading. Know that my specific examples, while powerful, will become

overused and useless almost immediately after this book is published.

2. People who get it but don't think creatively. They'll try to justify what they're already doing using the theory I've put forward in this book.

3. People who're advanced. You'll see the examples I provide as a way to illustrate the over-encompassing theory. You'll apply my concepts and develop your own systems of implementation for your industry on whatever scale you desire.

Software or specific aspects of social media may no longer exist when you read this book. Understand the theory behind what I'm saying and learn to apply it to whatever software you have available. It doesn't matter what aspects change – you'll be ready to adapt quicker than your competition.

250,000

Unknowingly, you've been building your list for as long as you've had Facebook. Some are close friends, some family, and some schoolmates you haven't seen for 20 years. These are your primary customers and your access point to thousands more. If I have 500 Facebook friends who all have 500 Facebook friends, that's 250,000 leads!

Unless you've already tapped this massive resource, don't start looking elsewhere to do your marketing. After all, these people already love and trust you.

The trick is to avoid coming off spammy. Posting messages on people's walls or tagging people in notes so that it appears on their public wall will get your feed blocked – quick.

Start with a simple "tip of the day scheme". Make it short and include a call to action at the bottom of each. Simply post it on your wall. The best tips are personal and no more than 3-4 lines. Highlight the tip as your "_____ Tip of the Day" and end each tip with, "If you have any questions always feel free to contact me". Here's an example:

Fitness Tip of the Day: Skin care is much better accomplished from what you ingest than what you place on top of your skin. Drinking water, taking fish oil and eating healthy fats like avocado and raw nuts trumps moisturizers any day. Feel free to message me if you or a friend ever has any fitness-related questions.

Even if you don't get responses, your tips will start to resonate with your loved ones. Within weeks I promise you'll be the one contacted with questions related to your tips. When your friends are ready to buy a product you're selling they'll buy it from you. As an added bonus they'll start sending you referrals if they hear of somebody interested in your business.

It's all a matter of becoming present in the feed — and your friends' minds.

Neighbourhood Expert

You've never heard of Maxim Zavet. He's a partner at Porco, Levy, Zavet LLP in Toronto, Ontario who specializes in real estate law. He's known in his world.

10 years ago Max would likely be working downtown. After years of hard work for a large firm he might have chosen to branch off and form his own company. Now, Maxim was able to leverage his tight social network right away and become the go-to guy when his friends need a real estate lawyer. Through constant updates via Twitter and Facebook he became the expert in his tight knit group. When somebody needs a real estate lawyer, they call Max.

Max still works hard but he's given himself the opportunity to build something for himself. Social media wasn't the only reason but it sure facilitated the process.

Don't get frustrated if your social group doesn't buy from you right away. Consistency is of the utmost importance. People will eventually come out and ask about your service. When they need what you're offering you'll be the first one they call.

How's My Writing Bru?

John Romaniello is blowing up. He's a skilled writer and knows a helluva lot about fitness. Aside from regularly appearing in every fitness magazine across the country, John just signed a lucrative 2-book deal. Add in the fact that he's got 100 distance coaching clients and a 6-month waiting list, and it's easy to see that John is taking over the fitness world.

When people share John's materials they speak a different language. They call the internet "interwebz" and sign off their messages with "talk soon bru". It's become a point of honour to speak like John.

When I asked John about the language he told me that he was just being himself. His goal is to make his readers feel like they're having a beer with him at Southern Hospitality in New York. John's one of the most popular fitness writers on the internet because he's genuine. He's created a culture around his blog that breeds commitment.

When somebody shares John's article you don't see the common "This article really helped me". Instead you'll likely see something like:

"Hey brus, check out this wicked article on training the back from my boy Roman"

People sharing articles gain social capital by showing that they're tight with Roman. After all, Roman's about as cool as it gets. Shares happen irrelevant of the information contained within the article. John's being himself and because of that some people resonate with him and become his people.

John's information is also high quality. He doesn't hold anything back when he writes, so readers and influencers in the industry have become comfortable trusting his material over time. He's managed to create an environment where followers look forward to sharing his material both to build social capital and pass on quality information.

John summed it up best when he said "People don't buy coaching, they buy coaches." How can you make yourself cool so that people want to buy you, not your product?

Pyramid of Quetzalcoatl

Arches date back as far as 200AD with the discovery of an arch at the Pyramid of Quetzalcoatl just North of Mexico City. They are one of the predominant structures in almost all civilization.

The arch can span a wide open space by applying a concept called arch configuration. The more compression on the arch the better as it holds the arch in a state of equilibrium. It's one of the strongest structures known to man.

Perhaps the most important aspect of arches is the ability of the concept to be applied to a wide variety of materials. Over time arches have been built successfully with an endless number of construction materials from stone to concrete to glass.

Facebook and Twitter will change. Who knows whether they'll be the prominent social network in 10, 20, or 100 years? Other networks will come in and out of vogue and the initiated will write books about the inner workings of each. The uninitiated will read and apply the systems like gospel without delving deeper into the theory of why information shares.

The specifics don't matter; leave that to the engineers. An arch works whether it's stone or concrete because the concept has stood the test of time. Human beings have the same needs as they've always had – to feel loved and part of a group.

Do you understand why the arch works or are you too swept up in knowing how much water needs to be mixed with the concrete?

Encyclopaedia Britannica

In March 2012, Enclyclopaedia Britannica announced it would no longer be printing books and an era ended.

I remember countless nights when I was young lying on the floor with a random volume I'd picked off the shelf. I distinctly remember leafing through Pa-Pj. I slipped through the golden-trimmed pages until I found a picture of a piranha. I spent the next hour learning every detail about piranhas.

Information used to be so valuable its edges were golden. Adults would buy books on instalments because they couldn't afford to pay for the collection up front. They'd proudly line their shelves with encyclopaedias as a sign of an educated household.

The joy wasn't in finding the answer. The joy was in the search.

Times changed and information became cheap. The CD-Rom compressed a collection of books into a disc that was portable. All of a sudden information lost its lustre. Clicking on a computer can never replace leafing through a meticulously crafted book. Information gathering became a need-to-know activity and learning ceased to be fun. A project was assigned, a mouse was clicked, and a plagiarized paper was handed in.

In a few short years CD burners came out, browsing speed increased, and storage space online grew. Wikipedia gave free access to more information than most people would ever need and bloggers all over the World started publishing their thoughts for free. Information that was once cherished quickly became ignored.

I'm not angry at the progression. It's part of our evolution. Information is no longer valuable. What you have to say is being said for free by 1000's of other people on the internet. Unless you're a leading researcher you have nothing profound to offer in terms of content.

What will make you succeed is how you package your content. How shareable it becomes. How much your readers connect with you, the author, and what they gain by passing on the information? The battle for content is over; anybody can rehash the facts. If you want to win the race to the top you must master context.

106,000,000

Search "SEO help" in Google and this is how many results you get. I went back as far as the 40th page and still found seemingly legitimate companies claiming to optimize your SEO with the promise to get you on the first page.

Would you go to an SEO company found on the 40th page of the search for help?

Promises of SEO help are everywhere. You can buy books on it in stores or download ebooks from 1000s of different sites. It seems to be the game that companies have to win in order to succeed in the modern day. I'd argue that this is old fashioned thinking. Search engines are being used less and less and the quality of viewers from search engines is poor.

SEO is important for some and not for others. Fact is, most web experts can make sure you have your tags in the right place and that's all I would suggest you have done. Quality customers aren't the ones who'll find you through search. They'll be referred to you through the feed.

The Local Gym

DCCcentres is a gym in downtown Toronto. They specialize in high quality strength and conditioning classes. With the help of a web strategist they found that the term "Toronto Strength and Conditioning" wasn't being taken with any authority. With some website tweaking and daily content (short and long) they shot up to first in Google's ranking. Search engine traffic is a large reason for the gym's success.

If DCCcentres tried to optimize their site for "Toronto fitness" they wouldn't have stood a chance. Instead they won the Google race for an abstract keyword that has a niche following. The people who find their gym don't compile a large percentage of the population but are solely interested in what DCCcentres has to offer. They're excited to find a place specifically for them even if it is through an organic search.

The gym is a local institution and doesn't spend much, if any, on print marketing. They've realized that they're a niche neighbourhood facility that appeals to a niche audience. For these types of businesses, SEO is valuable.

The nice thing for your small business is that I'd wager that much of your competition is also clueless when it comes to SEO. That means you have the opportunity to win your battle close to home. When researching this book I audited all the gyms close to my home and found that there wasn't a single one who had picked a small keyword.

Instead they picked "fitness", "exercise", "fat loss", or "personal trainer".

On the world wide web it doesn't make much sense for a neighbourhood company to rank for fitness. If however, they attempted to rank for "Toronto boutique fitness studio," they'd be #1. Anybody who wants a higher quality gym environment in Toronto would find them.

You're doing the hard work by maintaining a website and a blog. Stop buying books on SEO and stop writing your blog posts to rank better. Later in this book I'll show you how to write your posts for your audience. Think about what you do that makes you different. What type of people are specifically attracted to your services? They're the ones who will buy.

Once people find you, your next job is to give them the context to stay and spread your word.

SEOs Dying

Tony Gentilcore knows nothing about SEO. During an outside audit I was surprised at the number of simple SEO errors his site contained. Despite this Tony has become one of the most popular fitness bloggers around. His information spreads like wildfire and his audience grows daily.

Tony's been blogging since 2006 when an opportunity arose to provide some online content for the Boston Herald. He's a skilled writer, a knowledgeable fitness coach and one of the nicest guy's you'll ever meet. None of this is what's made him successful.

Tony has mastered the art of infotainment.

Take an article he wrote entitled "What Planning for a Dinner Party Can Tell You about Program Design". In it Tony describes the dinner party he and his girlfriend threw and how angry she was when he finished the meatballs. He joked about his girlfriend having to wear a HAZMAT suit to clean their apartment before guests arrived – a point we can all connect with.

The article slowly transitions to the lesson. In this case, the importance for personal trainers to focus on the major aspects of program design and not worry about the minutia. It's an important lesson but not a profound one.

I've read countless articles on the very subject but clicked off in the first 2 seconds due to boredom. He's realized that entertainment comes first, education second. The result is that when he makes a point people listen. This is how Tony became an expert. The same ideas that have been spoken about before all of a sudden become his.

People browse the internet to be entertained. If they want to learn they buy a textbook. If they want to know about plumbing they buy a "plumbing for dummies" book. The change is that wasting time online has become a stigma. The new wave of blog readers are embarrassed to admit they're wasting their time. Teaching them something while you entertain them will set you apart.

The trick is to find your balance. Tony's found his. What's yours?

1%

Search engines don't breed commitment, they breed carpenter ants.

For somebody in Tony's position, readers who find him via a search engine might be turned off. They won't get why so many people seem to care about his dinner party. Most will click off.

A 1% retention rate from search engine traffic is considered good. 1%??? The majority of people who find information via search engines are looking for specific information. They find an article, pick the specific info they need, and click off. They don't pay attention to the site or the author, and they definitely don't sign up for the newsletter.

Referred readers stick around. After all, they found your site because someone they trust shared it.

The Next Purple Cow

The idea behind a purple cow as described by Seth Godin is that it will grab your attention. Drive through a field of cows and you won't pay attention, but if one of those cows was purple you'd stop and have a look. To take it a step further, if for the next 5 miles all the fields were full of purple cows you wouldn't care anymore. You'd keep your eyes peeled for the next big thing.

The internet used to be different. Graphic designers could do beautiful things, and accessible and cheap information was something new and fantastical.

Now it's everywhere. The internet's turned into a field of purple cows. Everybody is trying to be different and nobody stops to snap a picture. Skilled graphic designers are present in every corner of the globe and information marketers are giving away more information on more subjects than anyone could ever consume in a lifetime.

Unique is good but it isn't enough. Why do people care about your uniqueness?

Lolcat

In the 1870s British portrait photographer Harry Pointer started superimposing funny text on pictures of cats. It took 200+ years for the phenomenon to catch on before the domain lolcats.com was registered on June 14, 2006.

An internet meme is an idea that spreads throughout the internet. It can take on many different forms; it can be a picture, hashtag, video, hyperlink, or misspelled text. Memes spread virally and have been the subject of research by marketers because of their potential to create mass brand awareness.

Lolcatz has been one of the most popular internet memes since the website was formed. They can be found on almost every website and are constantly shared via Facebook and other social networks. They're funny and make people smile but don't do much else.

A share doesn't help business if nobody cares who the original creator was. I'd take it one step further and argue that a share doesn't do any good for the business if the meme isn't related to the business.

Nobody cares who creates a lolcat photo. It's cute and passed around before finding its rightful place in the deepest depths of the internet. The only time it's brought up is when bloggers need a funny picture to keep their readers engaged. The blogger likely won't give proper attribution to the creator either.

The exception to this is if your business is a comedy website or, in the fitness world, if a motivational poster passes around for a workout webpage.

When creating photos to share ask yourself whether the person sharing them will care about the creator. If it isn't, the only result will be an increase in hosting fees from all the people clicking on and off your site to download the photo.

Viral Video

Videos share well. But is creating a viral video a sure-fire way to blow up a company or brand? I'm not convinced.

If you're a performer, then a viral video can make or break your career. What about other businesses? I was surprised at the instant drop-off in views on various YouTube channels that had been successful in hosting viral videos.

The pattern was always the same. 3,000-4,000 views on videos leading up to the viral one which reached 800,000+ (my criteria). After the one success views dropped back down to 500 each.

This pattern tells me two things:

1. A small percentage actually checkout the makers of the videos to see what they're all about. They watch 2-3 previous videos before clicking off.

2. Nobody cares about future projects if they're unrelated to the original video.

My suggestion is to look at video the same way you look at blog posts. Entertain first, but add in some education to show what your company or brand is about. The goal is to connect with your potential customer, not attract video carpenter ants.

Jack of All Trades

Pick one medium and make it your focus. If you want to write, create videos that support your blog. If you decide to make videos, use the blog posts to support the video.

Facebook

Right now, no feed is more important than Facebook. That may change but until it does I'd focus most of your resources to understanding and taking over the Facebook feed.

We all know the story, how Facebook started as a way for University students to connect with each other. Technology changes but concepts don't. It's not just university students who want to know what your relationship status is. It's also your friends, family, coworkers, and classmates from 20 years ago.

Facebook has become a tool to connect not just with old friends but also with like-minded people around the world – no matter how obscure their interests are.

Do you collect 19th century teddy bears? There's a page for that and you can find thousands around the world to talk about the newly discovered bear that was once owned by the royal family.

Are you an American Civil War buff? There's a page for that where groups organize get-togethers around the world.

Never has it been so easy for people with particular interests to connect with thousands of others just like them.

I'm not telling you anything new here. What you may not know is the untapped power contained in these groups. Members trust each other because they bond over an aspect of their life that used to isolate them. It's very personal and something that they're passionate about. When they share your word throughout their group, people listen.

Trust is a funny thing. It's all-encompassing. If I trust somebody as an expert on toy soldiers, it doesn't mean that I should trust them when it comes to insurance. Or does it? How else am I supposed to get a recommendation?

The New Search

Facebook has become the new search engine. More and more consumers are frustrated by the endless and often incomprehensible amount of information on the internet. Worst of all they don't know who to trust. Your quality product is getting lost in a sea of noise.

Word-of-mouth has always been the most effective form of marketing. The issue is that it was never scaleable – until now.

If somebody needs a plumber they're increasingly going to the feed because they trust the sources providing the information. It's easier putting a post on Facebook asking "Anybody know a good plumber?" than calling 15 of your friends or leafing through the yellow pages. Better yet the post reaches all 500+ of your Facebook friends while your phone call only reaches a few.

A plumber's job then becomes getting to the top of the feed for that friend group. It may take some out-of-the-box thinking but could be done for any small neighbourhood business.

My guess is that the plumber already has a strong friend network in their work neighbourhood. Why not start releasing a "Plumbing Tip of the Day" on Facebook? Make it quick tips that any homeowner can use immediately after reading. Have a call to action at the end asking the reader to contact you with any questions. Twice a week write a funny anecdote about plumbing on your website. Make something up if you want, it doesn't have to be real.

You'll find that other plumbers will be the first to share the info. When a post articulates what they think they'll share it to their list. Soon, handy homeowners will share your tips. All of a sudden your value and reach grows. This process compounds until you're the go-to for plumbing in your neighbourhood.

Now everybody knows you're a plumber. Your tips will constantly be in the feed because they're being shared by both plumbers and crafty homeowners. Anytime somebody is looking for a plumber in your expanded network they'll ask the friend who'd posted a tip about plumbing months earlier. Their friend will quickly send over your name. *All because you've been able to stay in the feed until a potential customer needs your services.*

The Guy

Everybody wants to know a guy. When somebody needs help with anything, doesn't it feel good when you can say that you know the perfect person for that? Social capital rises from being able to help others by knowing an expert. Being able to refer the go-to person, becomes a point of pride.

You need to become the guy.

The go-to.

The resident expert.

This is scaleable. There's a need for the guy for plumbing, the guy for furniture, the guy for fitness advice, and the guy for insurance. Whatever you do, there's a need for "a guy" and I suggest you make yourself the guy.

Gain the feed and this will happen. I'll show you how.

3hrs and 20min

That's the average time a post stays in the Facebook feed. It's your window of opportunity.

When somebody shares your status update you get another 3hrs and 20min. When somebody "likes" your status you get more time (depending on their relevance to you. I'll go over that in a bit).

So what happens in a bubble feed? Remember the flurry of activity that happens when somebody of influence posts an article?

Unfortunately that post doesn't gain much extra time in the feed. If 20 people share within 5 minutes, the length of time in the feed doesn't increase. The post becomes more prominent in the feed- that's important. But somebody who logs on 5 hours later won't ever see it.

The trick is to get your information to the top of the feed for longer.

I "like" this...

Nobody knows the specifics of Facebook's algorhythm. What I can tell you is that the programmers have gone to great lengths to try and figure out what and who you care about.

It's called relevance.

If you click on a link, view a picture, comment on a post, or share an article on Facebook, you're being tracked. Facebook will then prioritize future posts in an attempt to figure out what you care about and place them high up on your feed.

This is Facebook's attempt to deal with spammers and keep the site about personal circles of trust. If you feel somebody's spamming you then you have the ability to hide their feed and never hear from them again. If it's a close friend you avoid the embarrassment of de-friending them..

What it also means is that taking over the feed has never been easier. Become relevant to somebody and your information will consistantly appear at the top.

Relevance is the key to winning the race to the top. Facebook will change its algorhythm, but my guess is that they'll only figure out better ways to decide relevance.

How can you be more relevant to as many people as possible?

I also like that... and that... and that...

First and foremost, Facebook is a place to hang out. Continually posting information about your coffee shop is a surefire way to get your feed blocked. Write about your fair-trade coffee once a day. Spend the rest of the time gaining relevance.

I used to joke that a man's worth was solely determined by the number of likes his Facebook posts get. I now realize that this joke was one of the smartest things I've ever come up with.

The "like" button (or whatever Facebook has changed it to when you're reading this) is everything. It dictates relevance. Once you "like" a post, both the subject of the post and the person who posted it becomes more relevant to you.

The race to the top of the feed starts and ends with whoever gets the most likes. I realize that not everybody in my social group cares about fitness so fitness posts are about 1 in 3. The other posts are jokes, motivational quotes, thought-provoking stories, or personal funny stories. All are related to my primary goal – to become "the guy" for fitness even if they don't mention a thing about training. Here's examples of similar messages written from each different angle:

- Fitness: "The best personal trainers are those that realize the job is an art – not a science."

- Funny joke: "I was in the gym today and couldn't figure out what that buzzing sound was all around me. Then it hit me – I was doing dumbbell flys."

- Motivational quote: "Well, it may be all right in practice, but it will never work in theory" – Warren Buffet

- Thought-provoking story: "Today my client told me that she used a ladder to get a plate off the top shelf. I didn't realize why it was a big deal. Then she repeated "I got on a ladder". She went on to tell me that she hadn't been able to walk up a ladder in 20 years. It's not all about number goals, people. Sometimes the ah-ha moments are more meaningful than weight loss can ever be."

- "Personal funny story: I fell down the stairs at the gym today. Maybe that extra set of squats was a bad choice yesterday. Wow, my legs are sore."

The goal is to appeal to as many people as possible but not lose sight of your focus. Different people will "like", click on, and share different types of materials.

This is where most large companies go wrong. Their research tells them that one type of information shares best so they only create information in one way. The result is the same people share it and their relevance doesn't spread.

The problem is that some people will never share your material no matter what you do. How do you find the people wanting to share?

Who Shares?

Ben Bruno is the center of information in the fitness world. He publishes two lists weekly of the top blog posts and top videos from the fitness industry.

Right now Ben holds a lot of power. He dictates what gets read and what doesn't. Most bloggers try to get on his list. They're going about it all wrong.

They should care about who else is on the list.

Week by week I go through the list and add any bloggers I don't know to Facebook. I send them all a personal message saying that I enjoyed their material on "X" topic. My aim is always to build a relationship with them but they aren't my target.

I want to gain access to their feed. When I do I watch it like a hawk.

I'm looking to identify the people interacting with these bloggers. These are my targets because these are my Greg O'Hares and they will spread my word.

The pattern is always the same. There are 2-3 key people commenting and "liking" that seem to share every piece of content by the blogger. What surprised me is that the same names kept popping up on a number of different blogger's walls.

It became obvious to me that these people were building the paths to connect the fitness world with information. I needed to make them all fans of my work so they would share every piece of content I publish.

Slowly but surely I added each of them Facebook. Once they interacted with me on one of my posts I sent a private message thanking them for their support. This was all it took.

My wall is now a flurry of activity. I publish a post and it shoots to the top of the feed for a huge variety of people from fitness professionals to workout fanatics. The trick was not finding the influencers. It was finding the people who share the influencer's work.

I'd figured out how to attract the influential sharers in my industry. My next mission was to figure out how to stay in the feed for a longer period of time.

The Build Up

Spammers get blocked and ignored. The last thing you want to do is be labelled a spammer. So how do you get your material reposted throughout the day while only publishing it once yourself? Follow the few steps I outlined above and people will be sharing your material. Problem is they'll be sharing it all at once. You'll shoot to the top of the feed but you won't stay there.

What you need is a non-intrusive way of getting your material re-posted all day by others.

The day before you publish an article on your blog, do a post on Facebook to get your audience salivating. The best time is from 7:30-9pm as that's when Facebook tends to be busiest. Be creative. I've found that highlighting the problem and promising to answer it works well. Follow the post with a call to action, asking people to "like" the post if they want to be notified when the article's released. Here's an example for a post about a controversial ad that I published at www. thePTDC.com:

Tomorrow's post on the Personal Trainer Development Center is a great response to the now infamous Reebok/CrossFit ad. It's an important post for all personal trainers. Put a "like" on this post if you want to be notified when it drops.

This post had 161 likes and was viewed 8,214 times before the day was out.

The benefits are two-fold. First and most obvious is that your relevance goes up for everybody that "likes" your post for the future.

The trick and other benefit is that when you publish the article the next morning, tag every person who "liked" it the night before. I recommend doing it in the comments section so the person is alerted (tagging in the post shows up on the wall and labels you as a spammer quick).

The benefit is that people become alerted that they were tagged in a post whenever they log on – all throughout the day. When they do share the article they do it at different times so your post stays in the feed for longer.

The result is that you own the feed for the whole day – not just 3hrs and 20minutes.

Meat Snacks

When I was 14 I got paid $50 to sit in a room and eat meat snacks. It was a focus group to decide what shape and texture kids like. Problem was that I didn't like snack food and wouldn't have bought it irrelevant of the shape or texture.

I should never have been in that focus group.

Market research has never been so easy. Savvy marketers can easily assemble a focus group of their consumers and figure out what they want to hear. I can't imagine how much money the company paid to figure out I wasn't their target audience and I'm sure I wasn't the only one.

Your social network is your focus group. They're the people you're trying to sell your product to and they're the ones who will get your word out. Why not take all the resources you're currently spending on market research and develop these groups?

Better yet, why not explore and find an already established group similar to your company's interests. I did a simple search and found a teddy bear group with over 1,000,000 likes! I promise you can find a group of like-minded people no matter how obscure your interests are.

These are people who want to hear about your product or service and like to talk about it. If they don't like your idea they'll be silent, but they'll jump at the opportunity to speak their mind and show off their knowledge when given a chance.

Word about you or your company will spread while you're doing the market research. Bonus!

Romania

I recently had the Personal Trainer Development Center audited by an outside party. I'm about to undergo a major redesign and needed an un-biased analysis of the site. There was one major surprise.

Romania was the site's 3rd best source of traffic.

I expected the United States and Canada to be 1 and 2, but Romania beat out all the European countries and the fitness-crazed Australia. When I looked into it the reason became clear.

Livia Vaduva

One day I noticed her "like" a post and thought nothing of it. The next day there was another, and another, and another. Soon she started commenting on posts. This went on for weeks. The minute I posted anything I knew to expect a comment from her and I also responded. One day Livia sent me a long email.

It came at a horrible time.

I was inundated with emails and didn't want to read her life story. I'm happy I did. I was moved by what this amazing woman had gone through to become fit, and I stayed awake until 2am composing a response. Since then we've built up a great relationship.

When I told her about the stunning results of my site audit she wasn't surprised. It turned out she'd been posting every single article I publish onto the biggest Romanian workout group on the net. Talk about scaling!

The same people will comment and "like" your material. Your first inclination is to get frustrated. Don't. These are your most important followers whether you know them personally or not.

The push right now is to hire personal assistants to handle mundane tasks like answering emails and responding to basic inquires. Fight this all the way.

It surprises me how rarely I see other people respond to every comment made on their blog or Facebook. Isn't the goal of publishing material to get people to interact with you? Yet when they do you ignore them.

Automate and outsource other aspects of your life. Hire a personal chef and pay somebody to clean your house. I'd even go so far as to hire somebody to write my blog posts for me before I let somebody else respond to my emails.

Never automate your personal interaction. Your response may just get you posted on every workout forum in Romania.

The Personal Page

You have a choice.

Personal pages started as a way to connect with friends and family. Your closest followers are your friends and now, since Facebook has allowed subscriptions to personal pages, an unlimited number of people can follow you.

Facebook is great because it allows people to connect with you in a variety of ways. Some customers/followers will want to connect with you personally. They'll be voyeuristic and want to hear that you're going to hang out with your newborn niece. As long as you're careful what information you release, I don't see a problem with this. Industry celebrities must be in the spotlight more and more these days.

Ideas share from a personal page if they're written from the heart or personal experience. The lead-in is what generates interest. Here's an example from an article about a controversial ad:

> *"I don't cheat on my girlfriends or my workouts today on the Personal Trainer Development Center. Check out thePTDC's response to a controversial ad."*

I maintain two personal pages. One page has a pseudonym for my close friends and family, and the other uses my real name so everyone can find it.

Industry Leader

Being humble doesn't work if you want to set yourself apart. You must act like an industry leader. Al Ries and

Jack Trout describe the importance of positioning from a marketing standpoint. The same holds true if you want to place yourself at the top of the pyramid.

My guess is that a chain of command already exists within your industry. It's daunting to try and break through as an individual as the top is likely a tight knit group. Their power stems from their ability to pick and choose who the next generation is going to be.

Support them. Promote their materials and their companies and help spread their materials. And, then…

Position yourself on the same level.

After interacting back and forth through a couple tweets or facebook posts the top coach is now your friend – make sure everybody knows. When you promote their article the next day write something like "My good friend _____ just wrote this great piece on _____. Check it out!".

The person writing it will look past the fact that you're not actually a good friend because you're promoting their material. Slowly but surely all of your followers will notice you getting in tight with the in-crowd. Subconsciously you've put yourself on their level.

After a while the influencers will notice you supporting them and want to help you. You know you've done a good job if they call you a friend when they promote your content.

The Personal Professional Page

Professional pages are different from personal pages in that they're "liked". This means that an unlimited number of people can "like" a page but the page owner doesn't have to reciprocate.

The value of this has gone down since Facebook started allowing subscriptions. The way I see it, professional pages are followed by those who want to know about your business or brand.

Ideas share from a personal professional page if they're written straight-forward. In addition, a professional page is a great place to network and share the material of others you support. Here's an example of how I would post the same article about the controversial ad:

> *"Today thePTDC posted an article concerning the controversial ad supposedly released by Reebok/ CrossFit. Check it out and let me know what you think."*

The Business Professional Page

This is where you create your movement.

Most business pages have very little feedback. They're a long list of posts, articles, or news releases that are ignored because nobody cares. Having a contest to encourage people to "like" your page doesn't cut it anymore. The fan will "like" the page and hide your feed immediately.

Successful businesses are not those that just produce great products. They're ones whose customers care about their great products. The best way to achieve this is to give customers some ownership over the ideas.

"You be the trainer" is how thePTDC gets participation from its followers. Once a week I post a case study of a personal training client and ask for feedback on how to work with that client. Along with responding to everyone, we then post the best responses to our web site.

Ideas share from business professional pages by making the reader feel part of the movement. Here's how I posted that article on the controversial ad from thePTDC's business page:

"If you take personal training seriously you have to read this."

The Expert

You want to become the expert.

The theory of expertness is a fascinating thing. Why is a personal trainer who refines movement asked about nutrition? Why are niche experts within an industry expected to know everything about that industry?

If we accept that experts are expected to have advanced knowledge of everything pertaining to their field why do industry pundits encourage all up-and-comers to develop their niche? What is it that defines an expert?

People become experts when they have accomplished two things.

1. Support of industry influencers

2. A loyal tribe or following

Notice I didn't say that people actually have to be experts in their chosen field (this applies less in professional trades, of course). This is not the case. Some experts have advanced knowledge but most have hustled hard and convinced others that they deserve to be "the guy" for whatever group they decide to become an expert for.

The expert holds an unfathomable amount of power and it should be you.

How do you become the Expert?

Bret Contreras is a fitness expert. He's become one of the most popular writers and is featured in every major fitness magazine. In addition, his first book is being published in the coming months, and he's currently completing his PhD in biomechanics. Bret became an expert with less formal fitness education than you may think.

He was a high school math teacher with a master's degree. Being a workout fanatic, Bret built a garage gym and started training clients at home. He became fascinated with the Glutes when he realized how important they were for both performance and aesthetics.

Flash forward a couple years and Bret self-published his own studies and wrote an e-book entitled *Advanced Techniques in Glutei Maximi Strengthening*. That was his niche and it propelled him to expert status.

It wasn't long before Bret became known as an expert in all things fitness. Bret started on his PhD early in 2011, 2 years after rising to expert status.

It's easier than you think. The key is to fill a void.

What's missing from your industry? Is there an aspect that nobody has claimed expert status in yet? Think hard – this is your ticket.

Take your time to become an expert in one small area of your industry. Do you research and learn more than anybody else on one detail, obscure or not, of your industry. Once you've gained expert status you can call in your network to answer any questions you don't know.

True Power

True power doesn't come from knowing. It comes from knowing where to find.

It's easy to recognize when you've reached expert status as you'll start fielding questions unrelated to your niche. If you're a plumber specializing in kitchen faucets, you'll start getting questions about clogged toilets. If you're a real estate agent specializing in the urban condo market, you'll start getting questions about buying rural houses.

The assumption is that the expert knows everything, and while you don't you can leverage these questions as a way to strengthen your position.

Experts wield the power of the network. They have people on hand specifically to deal with various questions. The process becomes simple. When experts get questions they can't answer they simply "tag out" and let an appointed friend answer it.

Facebook makes this easy. Using the @ (note this may change by the time you read this) sign before somebody's name tags them in a post and notifies them that they're needed. The minute a paper salesman is asked a question about staplers he or she can call a friend who specializes in office supplies by "tagging them" to answer the question.

By leveraging their network experts accomplish two things:

1. They strengthen their position as "the guy" for information.

2. They strengthen their bond with the friend or colleague they "tag in" to answer the question.

The friend's social equity increases as they're given a chance to show off their knowledge.

Don't get frustrated and complain that people "don't get it" when they ask you a question unrelated to your specialty. Have a strong network and be willing to pass off responsibility to others. Help others and your position will get stronger.

The New York Times

One of the most fascinating developments in the past 10 years has been the emergence of the blog. What started as an obscure information source used primarily by early adopters has now become the most widespread and powerful source of information.

Some argue that blogs have killed the newspaper. I don't agree. Blogs have forced the newspapers to evolve, and the New York Times is a perfect example.

The newspaper has been continuously published since 1851 and has won an astounding 106 Pulitzer prizes. Throughout modern history it's been one of the most trusted sources of information in the world.

How interesting that the most popular content on the website is almost entirely the blogs. In fact on the "most popular" tab on nytimes.com the three headings are *Most E-Mailed*, *Most Viewed*, and *Most Blogged*. If it's clear to the newspapers what type of material readers prefer why are most companies still printing boring factual articles?

Heck, the New York Times even subscribes to Google Ads. Now I can get a ripped six pack while reading an editorial on the Republicans' position for the upcoming election.

Blogs started as a place where outsiders could ramble on about obscure points. Now, they are the primary source of information passage in the world. Most modern companies have accepted their need for a blog but don't know where to start.

Blogs are personal. Readers must relate and connect to the content. They must care.

Don't Start a Blog – Start a Movement

Why do you care about your company? What do your products mean to you? If you're writing for your personal brand, why are you so passionate about your chosen niche?

Never forget why you do what you do. If it's purely financial then either change your job or stop blogging – you'll never succeed.

Realize that you're not the only person who cares.

Personally, I'm passionate about improving the personal training industry. Instead of writing a blog instructing trainers how to train better I decided to start a movement. ThePTDC.com is a place where passionate trainers can gather and support each other. The power of the blog is in the idea, not the material.

What are you passionate about? Create your movement, and like-minded people will follow you.

Why Information Doesn't Spread

It's high quality.

High quality information stays dormant unless strong influencers share the material. Even then it's not read thoroughly on the internet. Save the high quality information for printed materials. Blogs are meant to be shared and enjoyed. They gather an audience interested in your product or service. This audience will purchase your high quality info when packaged properly.

Master the art of infotaining. Maybe your split should be 80% entertainment and 20% information, or 60/40.

Whatever your split, unless you have an emotional connection to what you're about to publish go back to the drawing board. Nobody will share your content if they were bored reading it.

The share button has become a way of the person pressing it to show off to their world what they want others to think of them. This means that profound information doesn't share well. Nobody wants to show off that they're ignorant towards a subject. This doesn't mean you're not helping them, it just means your message won't spread.

The Big Business Blog

A multi-national corporation needs to have multiple blogs, one for each facet of its business. Keep them small and personal and highlight key people in lower ranks of the business.

By highlighting sales or administrative employees of the month on the regional branch's blog, a company makes a valued employee feel special and adds a personal touch to their service.

It also gives the company an opportunity to acknowledge customers and encourage retention. Why not highlight a customer's business in your blog? You'll strengthen your relationship with that customer and maybe give them extra business which could lead to a bigger order for you.

The Small Business Blog

Stop your print marketing right now and put all of your resources into your blog.

You need to connect with your customers in ways that your bigger competitors cannot. This is through the personal touch. People will share your blog posts if you give them an opportunity to show off. Highlight your customer's successes even if they're unrelated to your business. When they pass on the post to their family and friends they're passing on your website.

Have a customer of the month and write up a story about your relationship.

Name an employee of the month and give some background on why they're special. Snap pictures of the employee working with valuable customers (with permission). You'll soon find customers coming into your shop or business congratulating the employee.

Be creative and write content lots of different ways. Make it personal and paint a picture of what it's like to work with your business. Why are you different and why should people care?

SEO Content

What's a more engaging title? "Tax help: a blog about tax help" or "How Jeff saved himself from the tax crisis and how you can too in 3 easy steps"?

I'd read the second article. Problem is SEO pundits will tell you to write the first because it ranks better in Google.

I know one thing about Google's algorhythm. They currently have a room filled with the most brilliant people on the planet figuring out how to enable good information to flourish. Their goal is to punish spammers and marketers with poor information. And you know what?

They're going to succeed.

Remember when you used to see Answers.com or Yahoo answers show up first in every Google search you did? When was the last time you saw either of these sites?

Google is optimizing for high quality content and lots of interaction. This is perfect if you're passionate about your subject. The best part is that they're making it harder and harder to cheat. If you want your message to get out it must be commented on, shared, and read by real people. Not bots and not outsourcing companies in India that will "like" your post 40 times for $20/month. (Yes, this stuff exists and it's more prevalent than you think.)

Moving forward, the only people needing serious SEO are small neighbourhood businesses, and even then it's just re-working of the tags and titles on their sites. If you're looking for somebody, send me an email. I don't get a commission; I just want to help good people succeed (jonathan@theptdc.com).

Add to this the obvious fact that you're writing content for your readers. The goal is to get them to share it with their trusted network. They're not going to share your spam, and the only people who will find it are the carpenter ants.

All Writers Have Egos

The time to be humble has passed.

You're the product. Remember John Romaniello from earlier? "*People buy coaches, they don't buy coaching.*" Well, people also buy plumbers, not plumbing. They buy financial advisors, not tax information.

People have chosen to read your material, you didn't force them. You're the expert. Your company is the best option. There is no second guessing.

A blog post with 3 tax tips isn't special. Any accountant can write that. A blog post about how you saved a client thousands of dollars is effective. Better yet, add a picture of the postcard they sent you from the vacation they can now afford. I'd hire you.

Show off. Speak about your past and why it's helped you develop your ideas. Talk specifically about the people you've helped. Be specific and paint a picture.

Why would anybody hire you if you don't believe in yourself?

But This Bread Looks Like a Giraffe – Not a Tiger

Sainsbury's is a company in the UK that manufactures a variety of groceries. One day they received an interesting letter. It came from a 3-year-old girl who decided that "Tiger bread" looked more like a Giraffe.

She gently suggested that the company rename the bread. This is how the letter looked:

Dear

Sainssssssssssssssssssssssbury's,

Why is tiger bread c\alled tiger bread?

It should be c\alled giraffe bread.

Love from Lily Robinson age 3½

The customer service manager agreed with Lily. He sent her a letter thanking her for the suggestion, included a gift card, and said the bread would be renamed. To top it off, he signed his name, Chris King (age 27 1/3).

The letter went viral. When it appeared on my Facebook feed it had over 27,000 shares! The story garnered international attention for the company.

Go out of your way for a customer and show a little personal touch no matter how small or large your company is, and you may just reap the benefits that Sainsbury's did.

I Want In

If you're in a position of power people will share your post in an attempt to climb the internet social ladder. It's a way of becoming part of a club and can be a powerful source of traffic for popular bloggers.

If you want to take advantage of this you have to project success.

Here are some tricks to make you appear bigger and more important than you are so that others will build you up.

1. Answer questions sent in by "readers" – Make them up. Say that you've been getting lots of questions about this topic and you wanted to respond. This creates the illusion that people are reaching out to you.

2. Reach out to well-known bloggers and ask permission to repost their old material giving them sole credit as the author and a link back to their site. Most industry experts have year's worth of old material that collects dust. They're ecstatic when somebody wants to republish it. Having them associated with your site makes you appear more important.

3. Cheat. While I don't recommend this option I do want to make you aware it's out there. There are lots of sites where you can buy Facebook and Twitter followers. It's relatively cheap and on first glance makes you appear to have lots of viewers. Don't expect any of these people to be active members of your community – I'd be surprised if any speak

English. They usually prefer to speak in 0's and 1's.

Being the expert is a position of power. Once you're there people will rush to join you. Be creative if you're having trouble moving up the ranks. Just make sure your content matches your status or you won't stay at the top for very long.

Boasting

Perhaps the most powerful reason why people share posts is to boast about what they already do. The internet's a funny place. Few people would email a friend to say they just came back from the gym, yet they're happy to post it on Facebook.

Look back on your previous posts and examine the results. How many people added value to the conversation. My guess is all of the responses were people speaking about how they would handle the situation.

The internet has given people an opportunity to show off like never before. People seem to gain great pleasure in bragging to the internet abyss.

Problem is few have the confidence to start the conversation themselves. This is where you come in. Give people an opportunity to boast and they will share your material as an extension of their thoughts.

Content doesn't need to be profound. The best content for sharing is controversial. The best example I can think of is women and weightlifting. It's a common myth that women bulk up if they lift weights. My readership knows this isn't the case and is frustrated this thinking still exists.

If I wanted to write a viral post, all I'd have to do is write 500 words on why women should lift weights. People have read it all 1000 times before – there's nothing new there. Yet, it gives my female weightlifting readership a voice. They show that they lift weights and are not bulky.

This concept applies no matter what business you're in. Figure out what the controversial topics are and where your audience sits on the issues. Write a short post detailing the argument and watch it pass around quicker than a Hollywood scoop.

Exclusion

Red Bull excludes most of the population in their marketing. They're extreme. Yet their energy drink flies off of the shelves even though it costs more than the competition.

If Red Bull tried to appeal to everybody they'd appeal to nobody. This is one of the secrets to their success. If you're into extreme sports you drink Red Bull.

Let's go back to your blog, err..... I mean your movement. Why do you care about it? Is it because you're fed up with other real estate agents ripping off their clients?

Exclude the bad real estate agents from reading your posts. Include lines like, "If you don't care about your clients, click off this site right now and never come back." Commitment level to your site will increase because now your content stands for something.

You can bet proud real estate agents who are fed up with the dishonestly in their industry will jump at the opportunity to share your material.

Action!

Nick Tumminello is a top strength coach who's built a killer reputation on the internet. So much so that he sold his business in Baltimore and moved to Florida to focus on developing his internet presence. He still trains select clients but has also signed a book deal, travels the globe speaking, and creates dvds and books sold via the internet. All from his beach-side apartment.

Nick's got one rule and I'm proud to say that, after speaking with him, I've adopted his rule.

Every post must have at least one actionable step that the reader can immediately take to solve the problem from the post.

Novel idea isn't it? Problem + solution = post. Makes sense to me.

Who are You Writing For?

Are you writing what you want to write or what you
think you should write?

Who are Your Viewers?

Anybody who reads your blog cares about you, not your
product. The purpose of a blog is to show your human
side even if you're a multinational corporation.

Write in the first person. Use *I* and *me* instead of
you or *your*. People connect with humans, not robots
who write generic information. They want to share
information that resonates with them,

Would you read and share something that's written
by a large impersonal corporation that given you no
reason to trust it?

Short and Sweet

Short material shares well. A quick tip or 400-word
passage quickly tells a story and solves a problem.

Less is more when it comes to blogs. Get in, get
dirty, make your point, and get out.

Reading on a computer gives me a headache. If I
feel something long is of value I'll print it out. Most of
your readers hate reading long-winded posts on the

computer. Once they trust you, they might start printing your material out. For the most part they'll skim and click off.

Lists

Jason Ferruggia is a strength coach in New Jersey. He owns Renegade Strength and Conditioning and has positioned himself as one of the premier underground conditioning specialists. Much of his widespread appeal comes from the massive exposure his website lists get.

His all-time most popular posts are his lists. Some of the titles are *Top 10 Ways to Improve Your Pull Ups*, *39 Ways to Not be Like Anyone Else*, and *12 Reasons You're Not Losing Fat*.

Jason's been able to leverage these lists to develop a massive audience. This provides exposure for his gym, the internet products he creates, a mastermind group, commissions from selling others products and advertisements from his website. That's 5 major sources of income, all benefits from his lists!

Perhaps the most important aspect of Jason's strategy is that every list directly correlates with an aspect of his business. I don't think it was a mistake that his massive list, *50 Renegade Nutrition Rules,* happened to get published a few short days after his book *The Renegade Diet* launched. (By the way, this post garnered 1000+ shares.)

Value

I can see you putting your hand up so let me answer your question before you ask it. Yes I agree it's difficult to offer sufficient value to your readers with short posts and lists. They share well and gain you an audience but they shouldn't comprise your only content.

When the Personal Trainer Development Center was starting out we had an issue. Our editorial material was better than most and our readers loved it. The problem was that they weren't sharing it. Numbers hardly increased. I needed to figure out a way to encourage readers to share the material, so I devised a new posting strategy.

Monday – Quick Tip 300 – 600 words

Tuesday – Full length article 1,000 – 2,000 words

Thursday – Full length article 1,000 – 2,000 words

Friday – List

In the first week of this new posting strategy there were so many page requests on thePTDC.com that we overloaded the server. Once we'd given our readers shareable material, they jumped at the opportunity to pass it on.

Longer articles provide value to your existing readers. Shorter posts and lists gain you new readers and customers. Learn to mix and match.

The Dreaded Blank Piece of Paper

There's nothing more intimidating than a blank page. Writing high quality blog posts is hard. Here's a great template for writing a quality post.

1. Tell a story (make it personal)

2. Highlight the problem from the story

3. Restate the problem in more general terms

4. Outline the steps to a solution

5. Conclusion.

A couple notes here.

First off, the conclusion is not a simple wrapup of the article. That's a copout. Leave the reader with some food for thought. A motivational phrase works well, as does wrapping up the story.

Next, in your story try to pick out obscure references for your reader can connect with. If you're speaking about a fat loss workout, joke about an infomercial from years back, like Jane Fonda. It'll give the reader something to laugh about and also open up the opportunity to end the post by relating back to the Jane Fonda workout.

Instead of staring at a blank piece of paper write down my 5 steps on a pad of paper. Fill them in, point form. Then, as you write, simply fill in the blanks. Bingo, bango, bongo – blog post!

Call to Action

Do you want your reader to buy your product after reading your blog post? Maybe you want them to enter your sales funnel by "liking" your Facebook page or signing up for your mailing list.

Always include 1-2 calls to action. Ask your reader to like your page or enter their email for more information.

How else are they supposed to know?

Deeper Down the Rabbit Hole

Want to really get down to details? If you're serious about getting your information shared take note of the following list.

- Monday is the start of the week so get it started right. Motivational posts and quick tips work well

- Friday culminates a week of hard work. So wrap up. Lists work well.

- Wednesday is work. People are generally busy on Wednesdays so it's not a great day to post

- Publish and market articles early in the morning. Breakfast time is a big window. Morning is a great time for information-rich posts as people are getting a start on their productive day

- Night time is for entertainment. Infotainment posts work well when published at night. Wait until after dinnertime. I've found 7:30-9pm to be the best time for posting.

- Sunday morning is a great time for weekly recaps. That's when a lot of people clear out their email inboxes and spend a couple hours on the computer.

I saw a Puddycat

It's amazing how many companies miss the point when it comes to Twitter. Twitter has single-handedly become the biggest contributor to information overload in the social media-driven world we live in.

Twitter's a place to hang out and get to know people in 140 characters or less. It's the perfect opportunity for your company to give itself a personality. The connections you make with other members of your industry or with your customers are invaluable.

Nobody will share your promotional material if they don't care about you first.

Feeds get ignored if they're constantly pushing articles, products, or services. Clients already buying from you follow you on Twitter because they want to get to know you. They already know about your products.

Follower count doesn't mean anything if nobody is reading and interacting with you. It can also be bought (the going rate is 1,000 followers for $5) so don't be tricked by huge followings boasted by others.

If somebody interacts with you make sure you send a response. The goal is to establish a connection. What's the point of being on social media if you don't foster interactions?

I recommend promoting your services once in every 8-10 tweets. The other tweets should be interesting observations, funny jokes related to your business, highlighting and promoting your customers, and compiling market research.

Market Research

Perhaps the biggest problem large companies face is that they are accused of not listening. Why not open up the floor to feedback once a day on Twitter? Have an employee monitor the feed and ask the simple question, "How are we doing today?" If you've just released a new product, ask for specific feedback on it. Get creative.

The anonymity that Twitter provides your customers ensures you'll get real feedback. It's a cheaper, quicker and bigger focus group than you could ever hope to get in a physical survey.

In a large company, separate Twitter accounts for each branch or department go a long way. Monitor these accounts and make sure your customers are following them.

Contests via Twitter encourage retention. Occasionally tweet out a 10% off discount code to be used by a certain date. Your sales will spike if people are paying attention to your feed.

Wanna Win an iPhone?

Noise! Twitter's full of it.

Tweet to a friend about an iPhone and you'll instantly receive 5 tweets from random accounts that tell you how to win an iPhone by clicking on a link.

Twitter accounts are hacked daily. Block users immediately and report them. The easiest way to identify spammers is to look at the user's statistics. If the account has 0 followers but has sent out 50-100 tweets it's likely spammer.

Information Broker

Adam Bornstein (@bornfitness) is the guy behind the scenes in the fitness world. He controls whose material becomes successful and whose doesn't. Twitter is his most powerful tool.

Adam is the editorial director for Livestrong.com and the former fitness editor for Men's Health Magazine. He has 20,000 followers on Twitter who all care about what he has to say. It's taken him years to build up his following.

When he re-tweets you can expect a flood of followers coming your way. If Adam decides to send a tweet promoting your content you can expect a couple hundred hits to your website.

This is power.

Everyone trying to make a name for themselves in the fitness industry wants to get on Adam's good side. He controls the feed. What he decides to promote rises to the top.

Look around your industry. Check a website called Listorious to find who the influencers are and start building relationships with them right away. It's worth your time and effort because one tweet from them promoting your services will spike your product sales.

Asking Questions

Want to get somebody to click on your link? Ask a question. Intrigue will help you stand out from the noise.

On a Facebook personal page make the question personal. An example using the same Reebook/CrossFit ad could be, "Did you guys see the alleged Reebok/CrossFit ad last week?" and follow up with the link to your article.

On a professional Facebook page use the question to strengthen your movement. Make people feel special for being part of it. An example using the same ad could be, "Why do you think the alleged Reebok/CrossFit ad affects us all?" and follow up with the link.

A promotional tweet takes the curiosity factor to a maximum. The twitter feed moves fast and if you don't grip readers right away you'll lose them. In your question you must give them a reason to care and intrigue them at the same time. Here's an example using the same article, "Do you consider yourself a professional?" and follow with the link.

Learn to stand out. Generate interest in every post while still appealing to your audience. Never forget that your followers care about you and your movement. They'll share your message if they feel it's an extension of them.

Intrigue

James (Smitty) Smith is the owner of Diesel Strength and Conditioning. He's one of the few that "gets it" and is profiting from a growing audience. These are people who anxiously await the release of his new DVDs and buy them the day they come out. His power stems from intrigue.

You won't believe this.

This will make you smile.

Bet you've never thought of this.

Smitty constantly boasts better open rates on his tweets and emails than other top information providers. He's developed a reputation for high quality content as people want to see what he's come up with next.

It seems that we're always searching for the next best thing. Your products are good, your services are high quality, and your information is top notch. Why not create some buzz around yourself?

What's Your Legacy?

Are you in this for the long term? Are you satisfied with a business or would you prefer a legacy?

Cheap products are sold with pressure sales and closing techniques. Companies providing poor service and low quality goods must focus on shoving a product in as many people's faces as possible with the hope that a small percentage buy.

These companies don't last. Nobody tells friends about them and word about their product won't spread. The products collect dust before showing up on Craigslist or on the buyer's lawn years later.

Your product is good. Your service is the best. You deserve a legacy.

Foster relationships and give your customers a reason to share. Help them succeed and you'll rise up to the top with them. Give your followers a reason to boast. Make them care about you and they'll spread the word.

They'll create your legacy for you.

The Power of Trust

Anthony Mychal is one of the best young fitness writers around. He's also a hustler and has managed his way into many of the biggest fitness sites on the net in a very short time.

After a year of writing for major publications he realized that he didn't have a following. Nobody knew who he was, and his social networks were a barren wasteland.

His problem was that nobody cared about him. They cared about the magazines he was writing for. Anthony updated his personal page only sporadically and he didn't interact with readers through any of the social networks.

An article of his would get published on a major site and a flood of visitors would be sent to his page. It didn't take long before he was back to 20 page views a day.

Soon after we spoke Anthony started paying attention to the bubble feed and found his own Greg O'Hares. He started developing relationships with his readers and developed his own methods of interacting with them. He's now an in-demand fitness writer and one of the most exciting young trainers in the industry,

Trade publications and media opportunities are great but realize that you are not the focus, the media outlet is. Don't bother approaching these institutions if you haven't established your funnel to capture the inevitable spike of followers that ensues.

Large media opportunities are a great way for people to hear about you but they don't care who you are yet. Stay up until 4am if need be to answer all your emails and messages. Offer a call to action for every person who contacts you to join your personal network.

Strike while the irons hot and go the extra 10%.

Traffic Sharing

Perhaps the most underutilized tool at the disposal of a budding expert is the niche bloggers that already exist within that industry.

Traffic sharing is an instant way to get people to care about you.

Popular bloggers have followers who trust them. They hold an insurmountable power over this following. If the blogger recommends they buy a book they buy it.

If the blogger recommends they "check out" somebody else's site, they do it..

The ensuing traffic to your site will be high quality. Readers and consumers immediately trust your product because they believe the blogger has integrity.

The question then is how do you get bloggers to share their traffic with you? Why you or your business?

On a Small Scale - Guest Posts

I'm not the first to recommend putting high quality guest posts on popular sites. I do go a step further though and tell you to concentrate on the blogger's audience and not the SEO benefits you gain from the link back (although that also helps). The most powerful sites for guest posts are personal ones – not organizational or magazine blogs.

A personal blogger's reach may not be big, but it is dedicated. Personal bloggers write most of their own material, and your guest post will stand out. All the posts in a magazine are guest contributions, so readers have become accustomed to guest authors and don't pay attention to them.

When popular bloggers allow guest posts on their sites they're sharing their audience. This is powerful. Followers notice you when bloggers they respect give you their seal of approval.

Build a relationship with bloggers first. Share their material and comment on their posts. Send them emails with insights into previous posts. Be specific when you pitch a guest post – tell bloggers why you think it will benefit their audience specifically.

Better yet, write a guest post and send it. You'd be surprised at how quickly bloggers jump at the opportunity to take a break from writing and post your content.

Enjoy the ensuing spike in traffic.

On a Large Scale – Sponsorships

Jaco is a fitness apparel company that blew up with a small budget. Its strategic marketing works.

Instead of taking the common route of TV and print ads, Jaco went out and identified the popular bloggers in their niche. In this case, it was a type of fitness called hybrid training. They then contacted and sponsored these bloggers.

The result is that Jaco is now the most popular fitness apparel in the fitness blogging community. It's hard to attend a workshop or symposium where one of the presenters isn't wearing their clothes. Heck, I'm wearing their shirt right now.

Of course the clothing is high quality, but so is the product of a lot of other companies. What set Jaco apart from the competition was that it found people consumers care about and got them on side.

Want word of your company to spread? Find the popular bloggers in your niche. Contact them - not with spam. Offer them your product for free and don't ask anything in return.

Instead of struggling to develop your audience, why not take advantage of somebody who's already done the work? Use the trust a relevant blogger has built up to get your company out there. It's the easiest way to get consumers to care about you.

Why Most Companies Will Fail

This information is not proven and never will be. The social media landscape changes too fast. The feeds will change before anybody can figure out what the ROI (Return On Investment) of a retweet or Facebook "like" is.

There are too many confounding factors and new methods being discovered every day. This is why I'm giving you theories and ideas in this book. I know the buttons will change, and often.

In big business it's easiest to follow the status quo. If you screw up trying something new, it's your butt on the line. If you work the way your company has always worked and it gets your company adequate results you keep your job.

One TV ad costs tens of thousands of dollars. Its intent is to appeal to a potential consumer's subconscious. I'm not even convinced that this was a good use of money years ago, but it's definitely not now in the generation of PVRs.

Why not reach out to people who have already become engaged in a community surrounding your product or service and gain their trust and support? They're out there – you just need to find them.

If you can't find a community, then you're in luck. You get to be first. Build the community yourself. I promise there are a lot of people who care deeply about what you do. There are plumbers and real estate agents out there looking for a voice. Be that voice and you position yourself at the top of the industry.

Stop doing the same thing as everybody else because you've all been doing it for years. Times have changed. Most won't adapt. If you do you'll blow past the competition and never look back. I challenge you to take the risk.

Cut your marketing budget and put that money towards a social media management team. It'll cost you the same as one commercial or a couple billboard ads. Develop a strong blog presence, create engaging content, give people a chance to show off, and interact with your customers.

Make Your Content easy to Share

If you work in a tight-knit neighbourhood there's no excuse for your material not to share.

Your daily or even weekly blog posts need to be short and specific. The goal isn't to appeal to everybody with every post. The goal is to write a post that hits home for a small percentage of your customers.

A plumbing blog should speak about one specific issue having to do with toilet maintenance one week and the difference between clay and pvc pipes the next. You'll attract the one or two people who are dealing with the specific issue and they'll call you for a job.

Also, people talk. Imagine how powerful it is if I write a post about low back pain and how to treat it. I speak specifically about a client I helped. I'm willing to bet that somebody reading my post knows someone who suffers from low back pain. They send my material on, and I have a quality lead.

Appealing to the masses is fine if you have lofty goals. For a neighbourhood company, though, blogs need to be personal and specific. Their aim is to appeal to a small minority of the neighbourhood.

How many customers do you really need for a neighbourhood business? Wouldn't you love to have a dedicated recurring clientele?

Show Your Value

Wouldn't it be nice if everyone who walks into your shop or visits your site is ready to buy?

Material that shares within personal social networks is special. You've somehow touched the people sharing it, and their loved ones notice. Instead of trying to persuade people to, "try out your product", you've shown them your value before they even come into your store.

Once your followers are ready to purchase, it then becomes a matter of showing them what to buy. Once they've bought you keep on giving them value and shareable material. Your network will grow day by day.

Make sure every post, every tweet, every Facebook comment has a call to action.

Soon you'll become the go-to for your product or service.

Gifting

When thePTDC.com released its free e-book entitled *101 Personal Trainer Mistakes*, it resulted in the biggest spike we'd ever seen. The site received 12,000 visits the first day and we were able to capture 2,500 email addresses in the first week.

When was the last time your company got 2,500 leads from dedicated consumers in a week?

The book cost $5 to produce (the cover design was done on fiverr.com) and took much less time to put together than you may think. I opened a Google spreadsheet and asked my network of top fitness professionals to send in any mistakes they've made on the job. Two weeks later I had a list of 120 mistakes. I sent the list out and asked people to write in solutions.

All I did was compile it into a word document and convert the whole thing to .pdf.

I could have sold the book. It's got tremendous value for any personal trainer looking to improve.

Instead I gifted it. The result was that it went viral. ThePTDC.com had passed 1,000 views a day twice before the book was released. It's never been below 1,000 views since. That book is largely responsible for the site's success. The massive shareability of the e-book created the base my site needed.

Most companies don't show appreciation to their customers. You're different. Show your customers they matter. Give them gifts. Do it right and you'll go viral.

The Power of Foursquare

Foursquare is software that simplifies this process for you. It's simple. When somebody "checks in" to a company, it's projected onto their Facebook for their friends to see. On the surface this seems like an invasion of privacy, but remember what I said about boasting.

People want to show off.. Instead of writing a Facebook post on their wall saying "off to the gym", why not encourage them to check in instead? A direct link to your company's Facebook page will appear.

Why not offer a free smoothie to everyone who checks into your gym? You're spending $2 in material cost to advertise to 500+ direct customers.

Restaurants can follow the same model. Offer a 10% discount on a meal or a free dessert when somebody checks in. The possibilities are endless, and the scale is massive.

Be creative and figure out a way to give as much as you can. Not everybody will share, but when some do your company will grow – and never look back.

Mark Zuckerberg, Andrew Mason, Matthew Mullenweg, Blake Ross, Naveen Selvadurai, and Peter Cashmore

You might not recognize all of these names but I promise you know what they've done. The above list is responsible for Facebook, Wordpress, Firefox, Foursquare, Mashable, and Groupon.

They've changed the world – and they're all under 30 years of age.

Never before has society been so controlled by the young. These (and others like them) are the puppeteers of the world economy. They decide what companies succeed and what companies don't because they dictate how information spreads.

Do you want to change the world? How about changing the business landscape in your community? It doesn't matter the scope, the concepts are the same. What used to work doesn't anymore. People who figure out how to get their content to share are the ruling class. There's no turning back.

Be the Guy

Take time to figure out what's missing in your industry. What niche hasn't been filled? That's your ticket to a legacy.

Start writing or producing videos on small details of that niche. It doesn't have to be profound. In fact, it shouldn't be. To become an industry pundit you must become the voice of those who don't have the confidence or drive to develop their own.

They'll share your material because it's an extension of their own thoughts. A way for them to show off what they believe and what they're proud of.

Soon you'll become the expert and your scope will spread. You harness the power. When somebody asks a question you call in others to answer it. Your social equity rises and you choose who you want to bring to the top with you.

Not everybody will need what you're selling right away but when they do – you're the guy.

You Need to Win the Race to the Top

The race to the bottom has been won in almost every industry. Trying to undercut your competition on price or quality is a surefire way to lose. The new race is to the top... of the feed.

SEO is becoming obsolete. It's saturated, expensive, difficult, and impersonal. A reader or customer who finds your company through Google pales in comparison to one that's referred to you. That's not new. What's new is how scaleable the process is.

The top of the feed is everything. The specifics of social media will change but it doesn't matter. Don't concern yourself with finding the next best tool for tracking metrics or buying books from a random "expert" on SEO. Instead, get yourself to the top of the feed – and to the top of people's minds.

People share as a way of expressing themselves and of showing gratitude, not altruism.

Give everything you have. Be bold. The safe route isn't safe anymore. Change your focus and put all of your resources into becoming a trusted resource. You'll soon be the voice of your customers and your industry.

The race to the bottom is over... Will you win the race to the top?

Afterward

This book is for the evolved thinker. It pains me to admit that many of you reading it will never act on the information you just read. So I challenge you.

I challenge you to act now because, if you found your way to this book, you're different. You have the passion to succeed and your product or service is better. What's stopping you is not major, no; it's that one annoying action step. It's that do or die moment where you have to press the button. Once you do, everything changes and there's no turning back.

It's scary. I've been there and I know. The reality is that if you want to race ahead of the competition you must be different. This means that you can't follow anybody else's model. There are no studies or statistics to fall back on. People will look at you like you're crazy. Your intuition is your most powerful tool, always follow it.

I wrote this book because I wanted to close the gap. There are too many people who have the skills to succeed but stop one step short. Social media has made it easy to get your word out; all it takes is the theory in this book and a little creativity.

Now stop reading and get out there. The top is yours. Make sure to email me at jonathan@theptdc.com when you get there.

Acknowledgements

I realize that this book is short. Short books are painfully difficult to write. Readers of thePTDC and all of my blogger friends were paramount in my decision to be brief. I didn't think it was fair to charge more for a longer book stuffed full of junk when your eyes are cluttered with so much junk already. So for you, I focused on the good stuff.

If you enjoyed *The Race to the Top* and are interested in or currently pursuing a career in fitness be sure to check out *Ignite the Fire: The Secrets of a Successful Personal Training Career* available on Amazon and Kindle also by Jonathan Goodman.

Visit www.theptdc.com or jonathangoodman.ca for more information… Be sure to say hi when you do.

About the Author

Jonathan Goodman didn't know what he was getting into when he delved into the blogosphere. His internet career started when, as a personal trainer, he first built a blog which he describes as "so bad my mother didn't even read it". As he went deeper down the rabbit hole he started to recognize trends and became obsessed. As the notebooks grew with research Jon started testing his theory of why information spreads on thePTDC.com (*the Personal Trainer Development Center*). The result was 5 website crashes within 3 weeks.

Right now Jon spends the bulk of his time in Toronto, Canada. He still acts as a personal trainer for a select clientele in addition to running the first free collaborative blogging resource for personal trainers. He also consults as a social media strategist for various large fitness groups. Finally Jon enjoys poking fun at the fitness industry in his weekly web comic entitled "Mighty Trainer".

Oh, and he occasionally decides to write books about the stuff he figures out.

At 26 years old Jon is a popular international "non-boring" speaker. To inquire about booking Jon to speak, contact **jonathan@theptdc.com.**

To keep up to date with Jon and sign up for his free newsletter go to **www.jonathangoodman.ca.**

2359655R00051

Printed in Great Britain
by Amazon.co.uk, Ltd.,
Marston Gate.